Testing Your Understanding
Practice Tests for

LIEBERT & SPIEGLER'S
PERSONALITY
STRATEGIES AND ISSUES

EIGHTH EDITION
AS REVISED BY LIEBERT & LIEBERT

D0070708

Robert M. Liebert
SUNY-Stony Brook

Lynn L. Liebert

Brooks/Cole Publishing Company
I(T)P® An International Thomson Publishing Company

Pacific Grove • Albany • Belmont • Bonn • Boston • Cincinnati • Detroit
Johannesburg • London • Madrid • Melbourne• Mexico City
New York • Paris • Singapore • Tokyo • Toronto • Washington

I(T)P The ITP logo is a registered trademark used herein under license.

For more information, contact:

BROOKS/COLE PUBLISHING COMPANY
511 Forest Lodge Road
Pacific Grove, CA 93950
USA

International Thomson Editores
Seneca 53
Col. Polanco
11560 México, D. F., México

International Thomson Publishing Europe
Berkshire House 168-173
High Holborn
London WC1V 7AA
England

International Thomson Publishing Japan
Hirakawacho Kyowa Building, 3F
2-2-1 Hirakawacho
Chiyoda-ku, Tokyo 102
Japan

Thomas Nelson Australia
102 Dodds Street
South Melbourne, 3205
Victoria, Australia

International Thomson Publishing Asia
221 Henderson Road
#05-10 Henderson Building
Singapore 0315

Nelson Canada
1120 Birchmount Road
418 Scarborough, Ontario
Canada M1K 5G4

International Thomson Publishing GmbH
Königswinterer Strasse
53227 Bonn
Germany

Printed in the United States of America

5 4 3 2

ISBN 0-534-34998-6

CONTENTS

USING THIS MANUAL

The purpose of this manual is to provide you with a means of testing your understanding of the material in Liebert and Spiegler's <u>Personality: Strategies and Issues, 8th edition</u>, revised by Robert M. Liebert and Lynn Langenbach Liebert. The manual consists of the following:

****<u>Chapter by chapter self-tests</u>, including true-false and recall items. Each item shows a page number in parenthesis at the end of the question, indicating the text page number on which the answer and related information can be found.

****<u>Key terms listed by chapter</u> following the self test items. Each of these key terms was introduced and defined in the chapter with which it is presented, and all can be found in the comprehensive glossary at the back of the text book.

****<u>Theorist and concepts matching self-tests for each of the four strategies discussed in the text</u>, to help you associate the major theorists with the ideas they introduced or developed.

****<u>A text-wide matching self-test</u> to help you associate major assessment procedures, techniques, and tests with those who created them or made use of them.

****<u>Answers</u> in the back of the manual, with explanatory notes to help you understand what is wrong with incorrect answers you have chosen, and what the correct facts are regarding the material covered by the question.

Self-testing is most useful when integrated into an overall study plan. The following sequence is recommended:

1. Study the material one chapter at a time.

2. Examine the outline at the beginning of each chapter before you read it, to get a sense of the chapter's organization.

3. Read the chapter carefully, noting the key terms (all of which appear in boldface in the text and appear, with definitions, in the Glossary at the back of the text). Pay particular attention to the unique ideas of each theorist.

4. Read the point-by-point summary at the end of each chapter.

5. Take the practice test for each chapter you have studied. If you come to an item about which you are uncertain, look up the answer in the text <u>before</u> answering it. (You don't want to "practice" any wrong answers.)

6. Score the practice test, using the answers in the back of this manual. Go over each item you missed and re-read the related material in the text until you understand why your first answer was wrong.

7. Use the matching tests to study for comprehensive examinations. As with the chapter tests, answers appear at the end of this manual.

Enjoy your journey into the field of personality!

CHAPTER ONE

True/False

1. Persona is the source of the English word personality. (4)

2. In the 1980s personality psychologists were finally able to agree on a single definition of personality. (5)

3. The ultimate goal of science is theory development. (6)

4. Theory, assessment, research, and applications (including personality-change techniques) are the four major issues confronting every strategy. (8)

5. Energy, natural selection, and anxiety are all examples of theoretical constructs. (9)

6. Testability is an absolute requirement of scientific theories. (12)

7. Correctness is the single most important criterion for evaluating theories. (13)

8. People often find bogus personality assessments very convincing. (15)

9. The rational approach is based on direct observation. (17)

10. Albert Bandura is a thorough-going determinist in his theory of personality. (19)

11. The nomothetic approach assumes that uniqueness is simply a function of general biological and psychological laws. (21)

12. The modern idea of personality and the concept of a "real person" is only about 200 years old. (4)

Recall

13. What are the two components of all scientific theories? (9)

14. What are the seven criteria for evaluating theories? (11-13)

15. What is explaining to a subject the purpose of and nature of research that he/she has participated in called? (29)

16. What are the two broad approaches to knowledge called? (17)

17. State or closely paraphrase "Murray's dictum." (20)

18. What are the two approaches to explaining the uniqueness of personality called? (20-21)

KEY TERMS

base rate	parsimony
coherence	persona
conprehensiveness	personality
control	personality change
debriefing	personality psychology
description	prediction
empirical validity	rational
empirical approach	rational approach
empirical research	relational propositions
history	scientific approach
hypotheses	scientific theory
idiographic approach	self-report
implicit theory	strategies
life records	testability
naturalistic observation	theoretical constructs
nomothetic approach	theory
paradigm	understanding

CHAPTER TWO

True/False

1. Correlational studies are mainly concerned with qualitative relationships, whereas experimental studies are concerned with quantitative relationships. (26)

2. Studies show that the relationship between TV violence and aggression is most likely caused by the tendency of aggressive children to seek out violent programs. (26-29)

3. Confidentiality and informed consent are two ideas central to the ethical conduct of psychological research, but there is no obligation to inform subjects of the outcome of research in which they have participated unless the research involves deception. (29)

4. The factor that is systematically manipulated in an experiment is called the dependent variable. (30)

5. Random assignment is sometimes carried out as matched random assignment in true experiments. (31)

6. The correlation coefficient can vary between -1.00 and +1.00. (33)

7. Temporal precedence is accepted as one criterion for causality. (37)

8. The stronger a correlational relationship the more circular it looks when plotted. (33-35)

9. Statistical significance always implies practical significance, and also shows that a result has been validated scientifically. (39)

10. The data from a case study are almost invariably quantitative. (40)

11. The case of Eve White is an example of a retrospective case study. (42)

12. When statistical analysis cannot be used, meta-analysis can often be used instead. (43)

13. The fact that nonsignificant results often go unreported is called the file drawer problem. (43)

5

14. Reliability is the technical name for validity. (45)

15. The MMPI can be used to produce a personality profile. (47)

16. The MAC scale of the MMPI-2 is a much better predictor of alcoholism than simply asking respondents whether they have used alcohol excessively. (49)

17. Nominations are used when only one rater is available to rate or rank subjects on a personality dimension. (50)

18. In general, faking on self-report personality inventories can only be detected imperfectly. (53)

19. Social desirability can be viewed either as a response set or as a response style. (53-55)

Recall

20. Name the three broad methods used in personality research. (26)

21. What are factors inadvertently allowed to co-vary with group assignment in a true experiment called? (30)

22. What are the two problems associated with attempting to draw causal inferences from correlational research called? (37)

23. What is the name given to any technique that combines and evaluates the results of a number of related studies? (43)

24. In a self-report inventory, what are the scales that provide information about eh trustworthiness of responses on the substantive scales (e.g., clinical scales) called? (46)

25. What is the name given to test-taking attitudes that influence one's answers but are not related to the actual content of self-report personality inventory items called? (53)

artificiality
case study
confounding variables
control
control group
correlation
correlation coefficient
correlational study
dependent variable
direct
directionality problem
empirical keying
experiment
experimental group
experimental method
file drawer problem
forced-choice inventory
independent variable
inverse
life history
matched random
assignment
meta-analysis
narrative

narrative
negative correlation
normative sample
norms
population
positive correlation
random assignment
ratings
reliability
response sets
response acquiescence
response deviation
response styles
sample
scatter diagram
self-report personality
inventory
statistical significance
systematic observation
temporal precedence
third-variable problem
time series designs
validity
variables

CHAPTER THREE

True/False

1. Freud was born with a caul. (63)

2. Altogether Freud wrote 10 books in his career, but only three of them are really well-known. (64-65)

3. Freud described three levels of consciousness. (66)

4. Jung agreed with Freud that sex was the only important human drive. (68)

5. Adler focused on the importance of striving for superiority. (69)

6. Freud believed that the mind works in symbols. (70)

7. Most psychoanalytic research is experimental. (71)

Recall

8. What are the names of the three mental structures of personality identified by Freud? List in the order in which they appear developmentally. (62)

9. What was the name of the first book Freud wrote in the 20th century? (65)

10. What are the three levels of consciousness identified by Freud? (66)

11. What is the name given in Freud's theory to sexual (or psychic) energy? (66)

12. What did Adler believe was the fundamental human motive? (69)

KEY TERMS

conscious

drive

ego

id

libido

object representations

object relations

preconscious

psychoanalysis

psychodynamic

repetition compulsion

striving for superiority

superego

symbol

symbols

unconscious

CHAPTER FOUR

True/False

1. Freud's dual theory of drives speaks of Eros and Thanatos. (76)

2. An alternative name for psychic energy is libidinal energy. (76)

3. The process of investing psychic energy is called catharsis. (77)

4. Freud divided personality into three structures: the id, the ego, and the superego. (78)

5. Freud believed that the preconscious was almost impossible for the person to access without the help of a therapist. (79)

6. Archetype is a theoretical construct introduced by Carl Jung. (80)

7. Dreaming is an example of secondary process. (83)

8. The superego is divided into two spheres: the conscience and the ego ideal. (85)

9. Freud distinguished six distinct types of anxiety. (87)

10. Repression is the only defense mechanism that is fully conscious. (88)

11. Sublimation is the most fundamental defense mechanism. (89)

12. Timidity and passivity may well be a reaction formation against aggressive impulses. (91)

13. Projective identification is another name for defensive identification. (94)

14. Denial is considered a relatively primitive defense mechanism. (95)

15. Oral sadism precedes oral eroticism for most people. (98)

16. Fixation may occur either because of frustration or because of overindulgence. (98)

17. Anal retentive characters are likely to be very messy. (102)

18. The female version of the Oedipus complex is called the Electra complex. (104)

19. The genital stage in girls parallels the phallic stage in boys. (105)

20. In his later years, Freud collaborated on many theoretical points with his wife, Anna Freud. (106)

21. The genital stage is characterized by heterosexual as opposed to autoerotic pleasure. (195)

Recall

22. What names did Freud give to the sex drive and the aggressive drive, respectively? (76)

23. What did Freud call the tendency to reduce tension immediately? (77)

24. What part of the mind did Freud say contained thoughts of which we are not immediately aware, but that can easily be brought to awareness? (79)

25. According to Jung, individuals think and act in ways common to all humans throughout the evolution of the species. What name did Jung give to this part of personality? (80)

26. According to Freud, which structures of personality are partly conscious, partly preconscious, and partly unconscious? (82)

27. According to Freud, if a needed object is not immediately available, the id is said to form a mental image of it. What is this process called? (83)

28. In contrast to the id's pleasure principle, the ego is said to operate according to what principle? (84)

29. What are the two aspects or spheres of the superego? (85)

30. Through what process does the child absorb and internalize the moral values of her/his same-sexed parent? (85)

31. Which defense mechanism did Freud consider the most fundamental? (88)

32. What is the name given to the defense mechanism which causes us to repeat or exaggerate a behavior that is the opposite of our "real" underlying impulses? (91)

33. What is the name of the defense mechanism originally suggested by Melanie Klein rather than by Freud? (94)

34. What name did Freud give to his sequence of developmental stages? (97)

35. Which character type is described as displaying extremes of optimism and pessimism? (99)

36. Persons said to be fixated at the anal sadistic phase of development are referred to as what character type? (101)

37. Which character type is said to be reckless, resolute, and self-assured? (105)

38. According to Anna Freud, what are the two major strategies used by adolescents to gain a sense of control? (106)

aggressive drive
anal expulsives
anal sadistic
anal retentives
anal erotic
anima
animus
archetypes
cathexis
collective unconscious
conscience
conscious ego
conscious
defensive identification
defensive projection
denial
depth psychology
determined
displacement
dual theory of drives
dynamic
ego
ego defense mechanisms
ego ideal
Electra complex
erogenous zones
factor analysis
fixation
genital stage
id
incorporation

intrapsychicconflict
ironic processes
latency
libidinal energy
moral anxiety
neurotic anxiety
objective anxiety
Oedipus complex
oral sadism
oral eroticism
oral stage
phallic character
pleasure principle
preconscious
primary process
projective-
  identification
psychic energy
psychosexual
rationalization
reaction formation
reality principle
reflex action
regression
repression
secondary process
sublimation
superego
unconscious
undoing

CHAPTER FIVE

True/False

1. Jung was the first to seriously discuss the midlife crisis. (110)

2. Erikson's theory of psychosocial development involves six separate stages.

3. Adler was the one who believed people dealt with inferiority feelings by compensating and even overcompensating. (116)

4. Murray identified a total of 14 basic human needs. (117)

5. McClelland is best known for studying the affiliation motive. (118)

6. Winter is best known for studying the power motive. (120)

7. The Hope of Power and the Fear of Power are highly (positively) correlated. (121)

8. Ego psychologists are more likely than object relations theorists to focus on adaptive behavior. (125)

9. Melanie Klein is considered the mother of interpersonal therapy (IPT). (127)

10. Five levels of object relations have been distinguished. (132)

11. Projective identification is a three-stage process. (133)

12. The first prominent psychoanalyst to express feminist views in response to Freud was Karen Horney. (134)

13. Heinz Kohut is known for his work on self psychology. (135)

14. John Bowlby pioneered work on attachment theory. (136)

15. Ambivalent attachment is also called disorganized attachment. (138)

16. Baumeister and Leary believe belongingness is a fundamental human need. (139)

Recall

17. According to Jung, through what process is the midlife crisis resolved? (110)

18. What name did Erikson give to the sequence of stages of personality development he postulated? (111)

19. Murray was the first to speak of a person-environment interaction. In his scheme, forces within the individual are called needs. What name did he give to the environmental forces that impinge on personality? (117)

20. People who prefer friends who are not popular or well-known are likely to be high in what kind of motivation? (122)

21. For Robert White, the central human motivation is for what? (125)

22. According to Sullivan, anxiety about the deterioration or loss of our relationships with others gives rise to what class of psychological processes? (127)

23. What is the name given by object relations theorists to the mental operation of dividing objects into their "good" and "bad" aspects? (130)

24. According to Horney, Freud's theory was based on one kind of model and her own theorizing was based on an alternative model. How did Horney characterize Freud's model? How did she characterize her own? (135)

25. Ainsworth identified four attachment styles. Name the style that is characterized by a failure to express distress on departure of the parent and then not moving toward the parent when he or she returns? (138)

ambivalent attachment
attachment
attachment theory
attachment style
avoidant attachment
disorganized attachment
good enough mother
individuation
inferiority complex
interpersonal-
  psychoanalysis
interpersonal therapy
  (IPT)
matriarchal
midlife crisis
mirroring

needs
object representation
patriarchal
personifications
projective-
  identification
psychosocial
secure base
secure attachment
security operations
selfobjects
separation-individuation
splitting

True/False

1. The "real" meaning of a dream is its manifest content. (145)

2. Freud believed that condensation and displacement are the major process in dream work. (146)

3. It is more correct to refer to projective techniques than to projective tests. (151)

4. Hermann Rorschach was the first to use a standard set of inkblots to assess personality. (153)

5. The TAT is concerned with identifying latent needs. (154)

6. Successful psychoanalysts almost never encounter resistance. (158)

7. Transference is a special form of resistance. (159)

8. The term given to a stable, cooperative relationship between patient and therapist is the therapeutic alliance. (161)

9. Interpersonal therapy (IPT) has been shown to be an effective treatment for depression. (162)

10. Many psychoanalytic concepts are poorly defined. (165)

11. In Freud's view, women are inferior to men. (167)

12. In his writings (spanning a period of more than 40 years) Freud wrote in detail about well over 100 cases. (169)

13. Freud's criterion for whether psychoanalysis had been successful depended almost entirely on eliminating the patient's initial symptoms. (170)

Recall

14. Freud distinguished two levels of dream content. Name them. (145)

15. For Freud, dreaming of climbing stairs is symbolic of what act? (147)

16. The TAT, the Rorschach, and the Draw-a-Person test are all examples of what type of assessment procedure? (151)

17. Breuer and Freud gave what name to the emotional release that often accompanies the conscious recall of a traumatic event from the past? (157)

18. Analysts may sometimes experience distorted displacements toward their patients. What name is given to this process? (159)

19. What type of orgasm did Freud believe was characteristic of sexual maturity in women? (168)

KEY TERMS

catharsis
condensation
countainer function of women
countertransference
day residues
displacement
dream work
free association
insight
interpersonal therapy (IPT)
latent content
manifest content
projective hypothesis
resistance
symbolization
therapeutic alliance
transference

CHAPTER SEVEN

True/False

1. According to Allport, dispositions vary in the degree to which they pervade a particular personality. (181)

2. A broad personality factor is typically called a facet. (184)

3. Dispositional psychologists are interested in demonstrating both intraindividual stability and interindividual variability. (187)

4. Dispositional personality assessment is most frequently described as multiplicative, because most traits tend to amplify each other when they occur together. (189)

5. The two formal criteria that have been adopted for measuring the adequacy of dispositional assessment procedures are convergent validity and discriminant validity. (189)

6. The special statistical technique most often used by dispositional psychologists is called factor analysis. (189)

7. The dispositional strategy is plagued by language problems. (183-184)

8. Most dispositions are skewed, such that most scores pile up on the low end of the continuum. (187)

9. Any given measure of personality will have a degree of "noise." (190)

10. More than any other strategy, the dispositional strategy is linked to drug treatment for mental disorders. (190)

Recall

11. The Roman physician Galen suggested what four personality types? (182)

12. What is the name given to a narrow element of personality of which broader elements of personality are comprised? (184)

13. What are the two formal criteria employed to measure the adequacy of a dispositional assessment procedure? (189)

KEY TERMS

convergent validity
discriminant validity
disposition
domain
enduring dispositions
Extraversion
facet
factor
Neuroticism
states
supertrait
temperament
theory of the four temperaments
trait
type

CHAPTER EIGHT

True/False

1. Marvin Goldfried is considered the founder of the dispositional strategy. (194)

2. Dispositional psychologists have used three basic approaches to identify the most basic or important traits and types: the lexical approach, the theoretical approach, and the statistical approach. (194)

3. According to Allport, a central disposition is one which dominates the entire personality of the individual. (196)

4. Allport's idiographic approach is reflected in his concept of patterned individuality. (197)

5. It appears that there are five distinctly different types of Type A individuals. (199)

6. Type A behavior patterns do not begin to appear until individuals are at least 16 years of age. (200)

7. Cattell identified three different sources of personality data. (201)

8. Factor analysis involves three separate steps. (202)

9. The correlation of a measure with a particular factor is called its factor loading. (203)

10. Cattell's Factor A appears to be nothing else than general intelligence. (206)

11. Eysenck developed the W-R-E-N model of personality. (207)

12. Eysenck was the first to identify the dimension called Extraversion-Introversion. (209)

13. The five-factor model is most closely associated with McCrae and Costa. (210)

14. Tellegen has argued that there are 9 (rather than five) "authentic dimensions of personality." (211)

15. The diagnostic scheme used by the American Psychiatric Association to classify mental disorders is called the CMD. (216)

16. The factors of the FFM are related to personality disorders, but not to clinical disorders (such as anxiety). (217)

17. The two broad classes of behavior problems are called externalizing disorders and internalizing disorders. (219)

18. Agreeableness is characterized by a preference for diversity. (221)

19. Of the supertraits, Conscientiousness appears to be the one that is most clearly heritable. (223)

20. Allport called his basic philosophy heuristic realism. (194)

Recall

21. What approach to dispositions assumes that the more important a disposition is, the more often it will be referred to in ordinary language? (194)

22. What name did Allport give to the relatively small number of dispositions that tend to be highly characteristic of a person? (196)

23. What terms did Cattell use to describe the three broad types of data that can inform us about personality? (201)

24. In factor analysis, what name is given to the table that shows the exact relationship between each measure and every other measure? (202)

25. What general name did Cattell give to the factors he considered the "building blocks" of personality? (204)

26. Name the three basic factors in Eysenck's model of personality. (207)

27. Name the five factors in the FFM model. (212)

28. The American Psychiatric Association has published a series of detailed manuals used to diagnose mental disorders. What is the name of this series? (216)

29. Which factor of the FFM is associated with physical fitness? (222)

KEY TERMS

cardinal disposition
central dispositions
common traits
convergent validity
correlation matrix
discriminant validity
disposition
DSM
DSM-III-R
DSM-IV
enduring dispositions
EPQ
evaluative
externalizing problems
Extraversion
extraverts
factor loading
factor analysis
factors
individual traits
internalizing problems
introverts

L-data
lexical approach
Neuroticism
Openness
patterned individuality
personality types
personality traits
Psychoticism
Q-data
secondary dispositions
social desirability
source traits
states
statistical approach
substantive
T-data
theoretical approach
theory of the four-
 temperaments
Type B
Type A behavior pattern
types

True/False

1. The earliest studies of physique and character were carried out by Aristotle. (228)

2. Endomorphs tend to be plump, where ectomorphs tend to be muscular. (229)

3. The peripheral nervous system is divided into autonomic and somatic divisions. (231-232)

4. There is a narrow gap, called the glial gap, between neurons. (232)

5. Hormones are technically called neuromodulators. (233-234)

6. Darwin's theory was based on an assumption of random mating, which we now know to be invalid. (235)

7. The "young male syndrome" refers to the fact that men in their 40s and 50s wish to be thought of as younger than they really are. (237)

8. The goal of most sperm is to fertilize the ovum. (238)

9. A person's overt characteristics, which presumably have a genetic basis, are called genotypes. (241)

10. Fraternal twins are dizygotic whereas identical twins are monozygotic. (242)

11. The heritability index can range from 0 to 100. (244)

12. The three distinct temperament types are sociability, emotionality, and activity level. (246)

13. Jeffrey Gray offered a biological theory of personality differences based on a distinction between the behavioral activation system and the behavioral inhibition system. (252)

14. Females are verbally as well as physically less aggressive than males. (255)

15. Marvin Zuckerman's work has focused on individual differences in what he termed sensation seeking. (256)

16. PKU is one of the few environmentally acquired dispositions. (259)

17. Eysenck believed that Neuroticism is learned primarily from the mother, which is why children in mother-absent homes tend to be less neurotic than those from father-absent homes. (250)

Recall

18. What name did William Sheldon give to the frail body type? (229)

19. The autonomic nervous system is divided into two parts. Name them. (232)

20. What name is given to the narrow gap that separates adjacent neurons? (232)

21. There are two types of steroid or sex hormones. Name them. (234)

22. What is the name given to the fact that humans actively choose mates, rather than mating randomly? (235)

23. How many <u>pairs</u> of chromosomes do normal humans possess? (241)

24. The mutual occurrence of a given characteristic or trait in related people is called by what name? (243)

25. What names are given to the three broad temperaments that can be identified and measured very early in life? (248)

KEY TERMS

ability scores
action potential
activity level
amygdala
androgens
approach behavior
ascending reticular-
 activating system
 (ARAS)

assortative mating
augmenting response
autonomic nervous system
autosomal
axons
behavioral activation-
 system (BAS)
behavioral inhibition-
 system (BIS)

behavioral genetics
biological evolution
central nervous system-
  (CNS)
cerebrotonia
chromosomes
concordance
cultural evolution
deoxyribonucleic acid-
  (DNA)
difficult
direct
dizygotic
dominance
ease of arousal
easy
ectomorpic
emotionality
endomorphic
estrogens
evolutionary processes
excitation
Extraversion
fraternal
genes
genetic similarity-
  theory
genetics
genotype
glial cells
heritability index
heritability
hormones
identical
impulsive-sensation-
  seeking (ImpSS)
incidence
inheritance
inhibition
intensity of arousal
mesomorphic
monoamine
monozygotic
multifactorial
neurochemistry
neuromodulators
neuron
neurotransmitters
parasympathetic nervous-
  system
pedigree analysis

peripheral nervous-
  system (PNS)
phenotype
phenylketonuria-
  (PKU)
physical
pituitary gland
polygenic
postsynaptic neuron
precursor chemicals
psychopathology
psychopharmacology
Psychoticism
recessive
reciprocal altruism
reuptake
seizures
sensation seeking
serotonin turnover
serotonin
sex-linked
slow to warm up
sociability
sociobiology
somatic nervous system
somatotonia
somatypes
stabilizing selection
steroid hormones
sympathetic nervous-
  system
synapse
temperaments
tempo
testosterone
theory of natural-
  selection
tryptophan
vigor
viscerotonia
young male syndrome
zygotes

CHAPTER TEN

True/False

1. Use of self-reports such as the MMPI for selecting job candidates was outlawed in 1978 in the case of McKenna v. Fargo. (265)

2. The NEO-PI-R is based on the seven-factor Model of personality. (265)

3. The NEO-PI-R encompasses 25 facets. (265)

4. The NEO-FFI is basically a short form of the NEO-PI-R. (266)

5. The Myers-Briggs Type Indicator (MBTI) has been out of favor for many years in the business world. (267)

6. Polygraphs are generally not admitted as "lie detectors" in U.S. Courts. (269)

7. Contemporary imaging techniques can be used in conjunction with psychological testing. (269-271)

8. Antabuse is most often used for the treatment of alcoholism. (272)

9. Electroconvulsive therapy is sometimes used as a last resort for the treatment of depression. (273)

10. Phototherapy has been found to be a pseudo-scientific treatment, with no evidence to support its effectiveness. (274)

11. Sleep deprivation is one major cause of depression. (274)

12. Scientists have recently succeeded in cloning a sheep, an accomplishment that raises many ethical issues. (275-277)

13. Coping styles may be considered stress moderators. (278)

14. The aspect of the Type A behavior pattern most clearly related to adverse health outcomes is cynical hostility. (279)

15. The Dispositional Strategy has the inability to predict individual behaviors as one of its major limitations. (281-282)

16. Factor analysis involves many subjective decisions. (285)

17. The great strength of the FFM is that it was entirely based on a well-established theory. (285-287)

18. Social desirability may be a serious problem with self-report personality questionnaires. (287)

Recall

19. What self-report personality inventory classifies individuals into 16 personality types and is widely accepted in business and industry? (267)

20. What is the name given to the most commonly used physiological measure of stress, fear, and/or anxiety? (268)

21. What class of drugs is most commonly used to control symptoms of schizophrenia? (272)

22. What is the name for the body's natural pain killers? (278)

23. What is the name of the one "personality ingredient" that seems to dispose individuals to cardiovascular disease and other forms of physical illness? (279)

KEY TERMS

antabuse
antidepressants
antimanics
antipsychotics
biogerontologists
computed tomography (CT)
cynical hostility
electroconvulsive-
   therapy (ECT)
endorphins
enucleated unfertilized-
   egg

galvanic skin response-
   (GSR)
gametes
gene therapy
health psychology
immune system
leukocyte
metatraits
natural killer cells
neuroleptics
phototherapy
polygraphs

positron emission-
  tomography (PET)
psychoactive
psychoneuroimmunology
psychosurgery
psychotherapeutic
psychotropic drugs
regional cerebral blood-
  flow (rCBF)
resonance imaging (MRI)
single photon emission-
  computerized-
  tomography (SPECT)
sleep deprivation
stress moderators
trait

CHAPTER ELEVEN

True/False

1. Environmental psychologists typically focus on covert behavior. (294)

2. The Environmental Strategy grew out of behaviorism. (294)

3. Behaviorism is a school of thought within psychology that can be traced to John B. Watson. (294)

4. The philosophical approach Watson prescribed was called methodological behaviorism. (295)

5. In classical conditioning, behavior is acquired and modified primarily through the consequences of one's actions. (295)

6. Environmental theories assume that most human behavior is acquired and sustained by some combination of the three basic learning processes. (296)

7. Much of what we (in contemporary Western cultures) consider masculine and feminine derives from social constructions. (297)

8. Environmental research is generally uncontrolled, so that natural environmental forces are permitted to operate without restriction. (298)

9. Environmental theory tends to use a large number of theoretical constructs. (299)

10. Environmental psychologists rely heavily on self-report data. (300)

11. Environmental personality-change procedures are commonly known as dynamic therapy. (302)

12. The terms discriminative stimulus and setting event are basically synonyms. (303)

13. In behavior therapy, all the treatment goes on within the actual therapy session. (303)

Recall

14. What is the name we now use to describe John Watson's philosophical approach to psychology? (295)

15. In the Environmental Strategy, what are the three broad types of learning that have been identified and discussed? (295)

16. What is the general name given to the personality-change procedures inspired by the Environmental Strategy? (302)

KEY TERMS

antecedents
behavior therapy
behaviorism
classical conditioning
consequences
covert
discriminative stimuli
interpersonal cues
maintaining conditions
methodological behaviorism
models
observational learning
operant conditioning
overt
radical behaviorism
setting events
situational cues
social constructions
social roles
target behavior
temporal cues

True/False

1. Classical conditioning was discovered by Ivan Pavlov, through the method of introspection. (308)

2. In classical conditioning, the UCS precedes the UCR. (309)

3. In classical conditioning, after a CR has been extinguished, it may later spontaneously reappear upon re-presentation of the CS. (310)

4. Garcia found that there are no circumstances in which a CS can be effective in rats for more than about 10-15 seconds, although a CS can be effective for as much as several minutes with humans. (313)

5. Voodoo may be explained by the nocebo effect. (314)

6. Drug-mirroring has also been called drug-mimicking. (315)

7. B. F. Skinner's name is synonymous with the operant tradition. (316)

8. Instrumental behavior was called respondent behavior by Skinner. (317)

9. Skinner rejected cumulative records (of the sort used by most other psychologists) in favor of noncumulative ones; this was to get an uncontaminated picture of the organism's rate of responding. (318)

10. Negative reinforcement is the technical name for punishment. (323)

11. A single-subject reversal design has two phases, the treatment phase and the reversal phase. (323-324)

12. Variable ratio schedules produce a "scalloped effect" when graphed. (327-328)

13. Richard Herrnstein developed matching theory. (331)

14. Behavior is said to be made possible by the presence of a setting event and made more likely by the presence of a discriminative stimulus. (332)

15. The opposite of generalization is singularization. (309)

16. Whereas operant behavior is elicited, respondent behavior is emitted. (317)

Recall

17. What method of trying to understand conditioning phenomena did Pavlov ban from his laboratory? (308)

18. In classical conditioning, the more similar the original CS is to the test stimulus, the more likely the CR is to be elicited by it. What term is given to this phenomenon? (310)

19. The effect of voodoo rituals may be explained by what effect? (314)

20. For repeated drug-users, their exposure to contextual stimuli along with experiencing actual drug effects may lead to two quite different (virtually opposite) effects. What are these two effects called? (315)

21. When a behavior that has been reinforced is no longer reinforced, the probability that the behavior in question will continue to occur is decreased. What is this phenomenon called? (318)

22. In the case of Robbie, the elementary school boy who frequently disrupted class activities and spent little time studying, what was the name of the design used to analyze the effects of reinforcement on his school-related behavior? (323)

23. When the baseline level of a particular behavior is at or near zero, what two techniques are most likely to be used to bring about the desired behavior so that it can be reinforced? (325)

24. Name the four basic schedules of intermittent reinforcement. (327)

25. The response rate of given behavior can be affected by the amount of reinforcement given for other behaviors. What is the name of the theory that anticipates this phenomenon? (331)

acquisition curves
acquisition
baseline
classical conditioning
conditioned response-
 (CR)
conditioned stimulus-
 (CS)
continuous reinforce-
 ment schedule
cumulative records
discrete
discrimination
discriminative stimuli
drug-mimicking
drug-mirroring
empirical definition
extinction curves
extinction
fading
fixed
fixed-interval schedule
fixed-ratio schedules
functional analyses
galvanic skin responses
generalization
gradient
intermittent reinforce-
 ment schedule
interval schedules
introspection
latent inhibition
matching theory
negative reinforcement
nocebo

operant conditioning
operant
operationally defined
placebo
positive reinforcement
punishment
ratio schedules
reactivity
reinforcement
reinforcers
reinforcing consequences
respondent
reversal phase
schedule of reinforce-
 ment
setting events
shaping
single-subject-
 reversal design
spontaneous recovery
stimulus control
time out
tolerance
unconditioned stimulus-
 (UCS)
unconditioned response-
 (UCR)
variable
variable-interval-
 schedules
variable-ratio schedules

CHAPTER THIRTEEN

True/False

1. The text describes observational learning as a three-stage process. (338-339)

2. Vicarious consequences are "indirect" consequences for the observer. (344)

3. Vicarious punishment decreases the likelihood the observer will perform the modeled behavior immediately but increases the probability that the observer will later remember the model's actions. (344)

4. Information value is a theoretical construct offered to explain how model characteristics influence observers' willingness to imitate a model. (346)

5. Gender roles are determined almost entirely by biology. (347)

6. Whereas the traditional model of masculinity-femininity was unidimensional, the contemporary view is bidimensional. (348)

7. Androgyny is a term commonly used now to refer to individuals high in both masculine and feminine traits. (349-350)

8. In general, the larger a person's immediate family, the worse off the person is in terms of verbal intelligence. (352)

9. The adverse effects of father-absence are almost entirely restricted to male children. (354)

10. A parent who is high in strictness-supervision and low in acceptance-involvement is employing a neglectful parenting style. (355)

11. There are four distinct kinds of family capital. (356)

12. The A-OK sign is universally recognized as an emblem signifying approval. (359)

13. In the United States people in a consultative relationship tend to stand between 4 and 8 feet of each other. (360)

Recall

14. Name the two psychologists who, working as a team, introduced the phrase "social learning theory" into the psychological literature. (338)

15. What theoretical construct has been used to explain that apparent pertinence of the model's characteristics to how the observer will respond to her/his behavior? (346)

16. What name is given to those individuals who display high levels of both stereotypically masculine and stereotypically feminine behavior? (349)

17. In general, the larger a person's immediate family, the worse off the person is in terms of verbal intelligence and certain other cognitive and social skills. What name is given to this finding? (352)

18. What are the two dimensions that give rise to the four styles of parenting (authoritarian, authoritative, indulgent, neglectful). (355)

19. Name the three kinds of environmental capital that have been described in the literature. (356)

20. What name is given to physical "signs" that have specific meanings that vary across cultures? (359)

21. What name is given to the specific environmental contexts in which cultural values are transmitted to others? (361)

KEY TERMS

acceptance
acquisition
activitiy settings
androgynous
authoritarian parents
authoritative parenting
behavioral repertoire
blended family
counter-imitation
covert
cross-sex types
culture
dilution effect
emblems

emic
enculturation
etic
exposure
familism
family configuration
financial capital
gender
gestures
human capital
imitation
indirect-
  counter-imitation
indirect imitation

indulgent parenting
information value
interpersonal space
live modeling
modeling cues
neglectful parenting
nuclear family
observational learning
parenting styles
personal space
remarried families
sex-type-
  undifferentiated
sex-typed
single-parent
social learning
social models
social capital
stepfamilies
symbolic modeling
vicarious punishment
vicarious consequences
vicarious reinforcement

CHAPTER FOURTEEN

True/False

1. Arthur C. Houts was the first to popularize the urine alarm for the treatment bed-wetting. (366)

2. Joseph Wolpe developed systematic desensitization. (368)

3. In contrast to reinforcement therapy, aversion therapy has been found to be totally ineffective. (370)

4. David Premack was the first to use a token economy with a real clinical population. (371)

5. Time out from positive reinforcement is a form of extinction therapy. (373)

6. Either prompting, shaping, or both may be used to increase the likelihood of an initially low probability behavior. (374)

7. Setting events are also called discriminative stimuli. (376)

8. Symbolic modeling is generally more efficient but less effective than live modeling. (377)

9. A coping model is one who never shows any fear. (379)

10. One of the greatest strengths of behavior therapy techniques is that all of them were initially derived from a set of well-established theoretical principles. 380-381)

11. The Environmental Strategy has been accused of making the logical error of affirming the consequent. (381)

12. The Environmental Strategy is the least deterministic of the four strategies discussed in the text. (381)

Recall

13. What name is given to the inability of people over the age of 4 to suppress urination while sleeping? (366)

14. What name is given to the form of therapy that creates a negative emotional reaction to a maladaptive behavior that the client experiences as pleasurable? (370)

15. What name is given to the principle that high-probability behaviors, even if they are not particularly enjoyable, can serve as reinforcers for low probability behaviors? (371)

16. What name is given to the therapy procedure in which a valued item or privilege is removed whenever a maladaptive behavior is performed? (374)

17. What are the two broad classes of behavior that have been successfully treated by modeling therapy? (377)

18. Because behavior is generated under a given set of circumstances every time does not mean it originally developed because of the same set of controlling conditions. What is the technical name for this logical error? (381)

19. What broad class of assessment procedures was employed during WW II by U.S. and British armed forces to select suitable officers for military intelligence assignments? (383)

KEY TERMS

anxiety hierarchy
aversion therapy
backup reinforcers
behavior rehearsal
coping model
deep-muscle relaxation
error of affirming the-
  consequent
extinction
imaginal
in vivo desensitiztion
in vivo exposure
mastery model

nocturnal enuresis
overcorrection
participant modeling
positive reinforcement-
  for appropriate-
  behavior
Premack principle
punishment
reinforcement therapies
response cost
self-modeling
skill deficits
systematic

desensitization
time out from positive-
 reinforcement
time out
token economy
vicarious extinction

CHAPTER FIFTEEN

True/False

1. According to the Representational Strategy, what is real to an individual is what is in that person's internal frame of reference. (392)

2. The columns of some ancient buildings were purposely built crooked so they would look straight. (393)

3. Humanistic psychology has played a central role in the Environmental Strategy. (396)

4. Kelly's theory is primarily concerned with self-actualization. (399)

5. Rogers and Maslow have both been concerned with self-actualization. (397)

6. The Representational Strategy emphasizes the importance of recovery of the past and putting it in perspective as the then-and-there. (398)

7. The Representational Strategy is characterized by the so-called nomographic approach. (399)

8. The name most closely associated with the existential movement in personality psychology is Carl Rogers. (400)

9. The Representational Strategy emphasizes the importance of sympathy for understanding the other person. (403)

10. A major theme of the Representational Strategy is its thorough-going determinism. (402)

11. Modern philosophers and contemporary scientists are now in full agreement that all important knowledge is objective. (392)

12. Rogers's theory may be said to be broader than Maslow's. (397)

Recall

13. What is real to the individual, according to the Representational Strategy, is what is in the individual's subjective world, which includes everything the person is aware of at a given point in time. What technical phrase is used to describe this idea? (392)

14. The so-called <u>third force</u> in psychology refers to what approach or intellectual movement? (396)

15. Who was the author of the book, <u>A Theory of Cognitive Dissonance</u>? (397)

16. The individual's momentary experience is referred to by what phrase? (398)

17. What is the name of the brand of psychology that Rollo May referred to as "an attitude toward therapy, not a set of techniques but a concern with the understanding of the structure of the human being and [her/his] experience"? (400)

18. Abandoning one's own connotation of various words and phrases and trying to understand what another person really means by what they say involves what psychological process on behalf of the listener? (401)

KEY TERMS

cognitive approach
empathy
existential psychology
here-and-now
humanism
humanistic psychology
idiographic
idiothetic
internal frame of reference
personal construct
phenomenological knowledge
self-actualization
social cognitive approach

CHAPTER SIXTEEN

True/False

1. According to Rogers, personality is mainly governed by the reality principle, not the pleasure principle (as Freud had argued). (406)

2. Positive regard is most valuable to us when we are praised or appreciated for doing something that is considered good and worthy by others. (408)

3. Rogers identified two broad classes of defensive processes: perceptual distortion and denial. (411)

4. Maslow suggested five broad need categories: the "highest" of these is self-esteem. (416)

5. According to Maslow, belongingness needs result from growth motivation. (419)

6. Maslow used the case-study method. (420)

7. Almost anyone might have a peak experience, though they are more common among self-actualizing individuals. (424)

8. Maslow considered <u>all</u> of the following historical individuals (among others) to be self-actualizing: Abraham Lincoln, Benjamin Franklin, George Washington Carver, and Harriet Tubman. (422)

9. Kelly's philosophical position was one he called constructive alternativism. (426)

10. Personal constructs are ordinarily continuous rather than dichotomous. (429-430)

11. In addition to his Fundamental Postulate, Kelly set forth 11 corollaries to his theory. (430)

12. According to Kelly, emotion is awareness of construct change; his definitions of specific emotions may be said to be value free. (432, 434)

13. Rogers believed that life satisfaction depends upon similarity between one's actual and ideal selves. (410)

14. What is the name given by Rogers to the inborn tendency of every individual to maintain or enhance herself/himself? (406)

15. What is the name Rogers gave to the process by which people evaluate each experience in terms of how well it maintains or enhances them? (407)

16. When the positive regard we receive from others is contingent on what we do, it is given what name? (407)

17. What name is given to the value placed on individuals' behavior by self or others? (409)

18. Rogers divided the self into two aspects. Name them. (410)

19. Ogilvie proposed that it is the discrepancy between what two concepts that determines the degree to which individuals feel satisfied with themselves? (410)

20. What term did Rogers give to the conscious or unconscious perception that there is incongruity in one's self-concept? (411)

21. Rogers divided defensive processes into two broad categories. Name them. (411)

22. What is the name Rogers gave to the process that restores consistency to the self-concept by reversing the process of defense so that the individual becomes aware of previously distorted or denied experiences? (413-414)

23. What term did Rogers apply to his approach when it was extended beyond the boundaries of psychotherapy? (414)

24. Name, in order from strongest to weakest, the five levels of fundamental human needs discussed by Maslow. (416)

25. Maslow distinguished two types of esteem needs. Name them. (418)

26. Maslow's first four levels of needs are said to be characterized by deficit motivation. In contrast, what process characterized self-actualization needs? (419)

27. What name did Maslow give to a brief, intense feeling that may include a sense of limitless horizons, of being simultaneously more powerful and more helpless than ever before, and of ecstacy, appreciation, and awe? (421)

28. According to Csikszentmihalyi, what is the name given to the condition in which people become so involved in an activity that nothing else seems to matter to them? (425)

29. What name did Kelly give to his overall philosophical position? (426)

30. What is the measure of the validity of a personal construct? (430)

31. The Commonality Corollary may be considered the "flip side" of which of Kelly's other corollaries? (432)

32. According to Kelly, which emotion is elicited when we become aware that an event lie's outside the range of convenience of any of our current constructs? (433)

33. According to Kelly, which emotion is elicited when we stray from a core role? (433)

KEY TERMS

actual self
actualizing tendency
belongingness needs
conditional positive regard
conditions of worth
congruence
construct system
constructive-alternativism
constructs
construe
deficit motivation
definition
denial
emotion
esteem from others

experience sampling-method
experience
extension
fully functioning person
growth motivation
guilt
instinctoid
organismic valuing-process
peak experience
perceptual distortion
person-centered approach
physiological
positive self-regard
positive regard
predictive efficiency

range of convenience
reintegration
safety needs
self
self-actualization
self-determination
self-esteem
threat
unconditional positive-
  regard

True/False

1. Another name for <u>schemas</u> is <u>knowledge structures</u>. (456)

2. The roots of the cognitive approach in psychology can be traced back to the writings of Edward Tolman, who believed that even laboratory animals could learn "cognitive maps" of their environments. (439)

3. Rotter called his approach a "social learning theory." (440)

4. According to Rotter, reinforcement value and expectancy are highly correlated; when one is high the other is almost invariably high, whereas when one is low the other is almost invariably low. (441)

5. Locus of control is an example of a specific expectancy. (442)

6. In general, as social class goes up, internal locus of control goes down. (443)

7. Shortly after divorce, many women become more internal in their locus of control. (445)

8. Albert Bandura began his career as a psychoanalyst, as did many other personality psychologists. (446)

9. Perceived self-efficacy is almost perfectly correlated with one's actual abilities. (447)

10. The higher a person's perceived self-efficacy, the less likely they are to go back to smoking once they have quit. (447-448)

11. According to Bandura, efficacy expectations stem from four major sources of information: performance accomplishments, vicarious experience, verbal persuasion, and emotional arousal. (448)

12. Perceived self-efficacy is a general trait of the person that is surprisingly consistent across almost all aspects of academic, athletic, and social performance. (449)

13. Mischel and Bandura both emphasized the importance of <u>person variables</u> in their theories. (446, 451)

14. Mischel argued that behavior is more likely to be cross-situationally consistent than temporally consistent. (452)

15. Cross-situational consistency is more likely in situations that require a low degree of competency. (455)

16. The most typical examples or instances of a schema are called prototypes. (457)

17. According to Hazel Markus, the cognitive structure one's self concept can be thought of as the person's self-schema. (459)

18. In 1890, William James speculated that each of us has three important "selves": a material self, a social self, a spiritual self. (460)

19. The ought self was first discussed by Rogers, and later picked up on by E. Tory Higgins. (461)

20. Self-handicapping involves acting in any way that increases our chances of success at a task. (464)

21. The evidence is clear that an accurate, objective evaluation of ourselves is the key ingredient in healthy psychological adjustment. (466-467)

22. Equifinality is a property of most goals, and implies that a goal can ordinarily be reached through any of a number of different means. (470)

23. Mischel argues that there are just three broad classes of important person variables. (453-454)

Recall

24. Rotter distinguished between two types of expectancies. What are these two types? (441)

25. According to Rotter, Reinforcement value x Expectancy = ? (442)

26. According to Bandura, our behavior is influenced by two broad factors. One of these is the environment. What is the other? (446)

27. What name did Bandura use to refer to one's estimate that a given action will result in a particular outcome? (447)

28. Most people construe themselves and others as quite stable in terms of their dispositions, yet research does <u>not</u> support this impression. What name did Mischel give to this seeming contradiction? (452)

29. What are the most typical examples of a schema category called? (457)

30. Markus distinguishes people in terms of whether they are _____ or _____ with respect to various traits or characteristics. (Fill in the blanks.) (459)

31. In 1890, William James distinguished three important "selves." Name them. (460)

32. From what does Linville claim high self-complexity protects the individual? (461)

33. People generally try to put themselves in a good light and misinterpret "ambiguous" information to their best advantage. What term is used to describe this phenomenon? (464)

34. We process information about past experiences selectively, in a way that is consistent with our current mood. Thus, according to Wright and Mischel, people tend to have a _____
_____. (Fill in the appropriate phrase.)
(466)

35. Most goals can be satisfied in more than one way. This reflects what property of goals? (470)

KEY TERMS

actual self
aschematic
behavior potential
behavioral signatures-
 of personality
cognitive dissonance
competencies

consistency paradox
cross-situational-
 consistency
efficacy expectations
emotional arousal
encoding strategies
expectancies

expectancy
external locus of-
 control
generalized expectancy
goal content
goals
ideal self
internal locus of-
 control
locus of control
material self
mood-congruent bias
ought self
outcome expectations
perceived self-efficacy
performance-
 accomplishments
person variables
personal life story
personal value
personal constructs
personality variables
personality coefficient
plans
possible selves
proprium
prototypes
psychological situation
reinforcement value
schemas
schematic
self
self-complexity
self-efficacy
self-enhancement
self-esteem
self-handicapping
self-monitoring
self-regulatory systems
self-schema
social self
specific expectancy
spiritual self
temporal consistency
theory of-
 perceived-efficacy
triadic reciprocal-
 determinism
verbal persuasion
vicarious experience
working self-concept

CHAPTER EIGHTEEN

True/False

1. A major goal of the Representational Strategy, and particularly of the phenomenological approach, is to gain <u>empathic understanding</u> of the individual being assessed. (476)

2. The Q-sort is a standardized procedure for assessing the self-concept. (476)

3. Personal constructs are most frequently assessed by the NEO-PI and the NEO-PI-R. (477)

4. The Rep test uses a grid to organize and sort information by the subject. (478)

5. Locus of control is most frequently assessed by the L-C scale. (479)

6. Rogers called his form of therapy person-centered. (480)

7. The most important role played by the Rogerian therapist is to supply conditions of worth for the client. (481)

8. The two basic techniques of the Rogerian therapist are clarification of feelings and restatement of content; of these, clarification of feelings is the more important. (482)

9. Fixed-role therapy was developed by Carolin Showers. (482)

10. Bandura has hypothesized that all forms of therapy work through strengthening the client's perceived self-efficacy. (483)

11. Modeling is generally less effective than verbal persuasion, because the latter emphasizes the importance of performance accomplishments. (484)

12. Cognitive therapy focuses entirely on cognitions; the idea of behaviorally-based techniques such as graded task assignments is assumed to be irrelevant to underlying cognitions and typically cause clients to abandon therapy prematurely. (487)

13. Meichenbaum demonstrated that self-instructional training may be a powerful cognitive-behavioral therapy technique. (488)

14. Problem-solving therapy was developed by Walter Mischel, as a result of his studies on how children solve problems. (489)

15. The Representational Strategy is the only strategy that manages to avoid circular reasoning completely. (496)

16. Maslow may have overestimated the degree to which safety needs are met by people in technologically advanced countries. (417)

17. The Representational Strategy has been accused of giving inadequate coverage to personality development. (496)

18. Representational personality assessment generally assumes that people are aware of most of their feelings, whereas the Psychoanalytic Strategy doubts this assumption. (498)

19. Freud's theory may be said to have focused on the seedy side of human nature; the Representational Strategy, by contrast, has been accused of taking an overly optimistic and even "romantic" view of the human condition. (499)

Recall

20. What is the name of the standardized procedure Rogers used for assessing the self-concept? (476)

21. What is the name of the test Kelly used to identify an individual's personal constructs? (477)

22. Rogers originally referred to his brand of therapy as <u>client-centered</u> therapy. He later renamed it. What was the new name he used? (480)

23. What is the name Kelly gave to his own brand of therapy? (482)

24. What is the name given to the assessment procedure in which people are asked to perform a series of tasks requiring increasingly more feared interactions with a feared object or situation? (484)

25. What is the name of the substance that blocks the effect of the body's natural pain killers? (485)

26. Name the two psychologists who devised problem-solving therapy. (489)

27. In treating marital discord, couples may be asked to increase the number of positive behaviors they display toward each other each day. What is the name given to this technique of treatment? (491)

KEY TERMS

behavioral avoidance test
caring-days technique
clarification of feelings
cognitive participant modeling
cognitive restructuring
cognitive modeling
cognitive therapies
congitive therapy
covert self-instruction
empathic understanding
fading
fixed-role sketch
fixed-role therapy
graded task assignments
I-E scale
overt self-instruction
person-centered therapy
problem-solving therapy
restatement of content
role construct repertory test (Rep test)
self-instructional training
self-statements
self-talk

CHAPTER NINETEEN

True/False

1. The general movement in personality psychology over the past few decades has been toward unification. (506)

2. Although Freud was once the most influential personality psychologist, it now appears that Thomas D'Zurilla has taken over that role. (507)

3. Freudian slips have now been shown to almost never occur, probably because the modern mind is too rational and cognitive to produce them. (507)

4. There are clear parallel's between the Freudian defense mechanisms and those suggested by Carl Rogers. (508)

5. Freud denied that natural selection played any significant role in personality, though he acknowledged its effects on lower life forms. (508)

6. The term cognitive-behavioral is rapidly losing its appeal, as it becomes more evident that the only way to produce lasting changes in personality is through psychotropic medication. (509)

7. Schools of psychotherapy are now much more divergent and separated than they were in the 1950s; this is due to significant advances in each of the strategies, to make them more sharply distinct from any of the others. (509-510)

8. The idionomic approach allows researchers to appreciate the uniqueness of each individual, while still seeking general laws applicable to all human behavior. (511)

9. Dispositional psychologists remain wary of attaching "deeper meaning" to any personality phenomena. (512)

10. The state of "flow" has been described in greatest detail by Mihaly Csikszentmihalyi. (513)

11. As the 21st century begins, it is clear that the search for a full understanding of human personality will be scientifically complete within the next 10 or 15 years at the most. (514)

Recall

12. Wegner postulates that any attempt to control one's own mind involves two opposing processes. Name them. (507)

13. <u>Cognitive-behavioral</u> is a term used quite often by psychologists these days, especially in reference to therapy. This reflects growing overlap of which two strategies? (509)

14. What is the name of the approach that attempts to allow for attention to individuals and appreciate their uniqueness while still permitting some group comparisons and generalizable conclusions? (509)

MATCHING THEORISTS AND THEIR IDEAS--PART II
                THE PSYCHOANALYTIC STRATEGY

1. Id, Ego, Superego	a.	Adler
2. Archetypes	b.	Ainsworth
3. Midlife Crisis	c.	Baumeister & Leary
4. Basic Trust vs. Mistrust	d.	Bowlby
5. Psychosocial Stages of Development	e.	Erikson
6. Psychosexual Stages of Development	f.	Freud
7. Inferiority Complex	g.	Hartmann
8. Needs and Press	h.	Horney
9. Achievement Motivation	i.	Jung
10. The Power Motive	j.	Klein
11. Adaptive Functions of the Ego	k.	Kohut
12. Competence Motivation	l.	Mahler
13. Five Levels of Object Relations	m.	McClelland
14. Personifications	n.	Murray
15. Separation-Individuation	o.	Sullivan
16. Five Levels of Object Relations	p.	Westen
17. Feminist Reaction to Freud	q.	White
18. Self Psychology	r.	Winter
19. Attachment Theory		
20. Styles of Attachment		
21. Belongingness as a Fundamental Need		
22. Displacement		
23. Countertransference		
24. Interpersonal Therapy (IPT)		

MATCHING THEORISTS AND THEIR IDEAS--PART III
THE DISPOSITIONAL STRATEGY

1. Heuristic Realism
2. Cardinal Disposition
3. Type A Behavior Pattern
4. L-data
5. Source Traits
6. Psychoticism
7. Five-factor Model (FFM)
8. Seven-factor Model
9. Conscientiousness
10. Intelligence as Personality Trait
11. <u>Physique and Character</u>
12. Mesomorphic
13. Cerebrotonia
14. Natural Selection
15. "Young Male" Syndrome
16. Sperm Wars
17. Behavioral Activation System (BAS)
18. Sensation Seeking
19. Metatraits
20. Premature Acceptance of the FFM

a. Allport
b. Baker & Bellis
c. Baumeister
d. Block
e. Cattell
f. Costa & McCrae
g. Darwin
h. Eysenck
i. Friedman & Rosenman
j. Gray
k. Kretschmer
l. Sheldon
m. Tellegen & Waller
n. Wilson & Daly
o. Zuckerman

MATCHING THEORISTS AND THEIR IDEAS--PART IV
THE ENVIRONMENTAL STRATEGY

1. Father of Behaviorism

2. Operant Conditioning

3. Classical Conditioning

4. "Preparedness" in
   Classical Conditioning

5. Cumulative Records

6. Matching Theory

7. Acquisition-Performance
   Distinction

8. Parenting Styles

9. Urine Alarm

10. Systematic Desensitization

a. Bandura

b. Baumrind

c. Garcia

d. Herrnstein

e. Mowrer &
   Mowrer

f. Pavlov

g. Skinner

h. Watson

i. Wolpe

j. Premack

k. Rachlin

MATCHING THEORISTS AND THEIR IDEAS--PART V
THE REPRESENTATIONAL STRATEGY

1. Personal Constructs
2. Existential Psychology
3. Actualizing Tendency
4. Undesirable Self-concept
5. Need Hierarchy
6. Deficit Motivation
7. Peak Experience
8. Flow
9. Predictive Efficiency
10. Range of Convenience
11. Behavior Potential
12. Triadic Reciprocal Determinism
13. Personality Coefficient
14. Consistency Paradox
15. Behavioral Signatures of Personality
16. Schematic vs. Aschematic
17. Ought Self
18. Emotional Spillover

a. Bandura
b. Csikszent-
   mihalyi
c. Higgins
d. Kelly
e. Linville
f. Markus
g. Maslow
h. May
i. Mischel
j. Ogilvie
k. Rogers
l. Rotter
m. D'Zurilla
n. Spiegler

MATCHING ASSESSMENT PROCEDURES AND THEIR CREATORS

1. Q-sort

2. Rep Test

3. I-E Scale

4. Experience Sampling Method

5. EPQ

6. NEO-PI

7. Free Association

8. Inkblots

a. Costa &
   McCrae

b. Csikszent-
   mihalyi

c. Eysenck

d. Freud

e. Kelly

f. Rogers

g. Rorschach

h. Rotter

CHAPTER ONE

1. T
2. F
3. T
4. T
5. T
6. T
7. F
8. T
9. F
10. F
11. T
12. T

13. Theoretical constructs, relational propositions

14. Empirical validity, parsimony, comprehensiveness, coherence, testability, usefulness, acceptability

15. Debriefing

16. Rational approach, empirical approach

17. In some ways each person is like all other persons; in some ways each person is like some other persons; in some ways each person is like no other persons.

1.	F	
2.	F	
3.	F	
4.	F	
5.	T	
6.	T	
7.	T	
8.	F	
9.	F	
10.	F	
11.	F	
12.	F	
13.	T	
14.	F	
15.	T	
16.	F	
17.	F	
18.	T	
19.	T	

20. Experimental, correlational, case-study

21. confounding variables

22. Directionality problem, third variable problem

23. Meta-analysis

24. Validity scales

25. Response sets

CHAPTER THREE

1. T

2. F

3. T

4. F

5. T

6. T

7. F

8. Id, ego, superego

9. <u>Interpretation of Dreams</u>

10. Conscious, preconscious, unconscious

11. Libido

12. Striving for superiority

1. T	19. F
2. T	20. F (Anna was Freud's daughter)
3. F (Cathexis)	
4. T	21. T
5. F	22. Eros, Thanatos
6. T	
7. F (Primary process)	23. Pleasure principle
	24. Preconscious
8. T	
9. F (Three types: neurotic anxiety, moral anxiety, objective anxiety)	25. Collective unconscious
	26. Ego and superego
	27. Primary process or wish fulfillment
10. F (No defense mechanism is conscious)	
	28. Reality principle
11. F	
	29. Ego ideal, conscience
12. T	
13. F	30. Defensive identification or incorporation
14. T	
15. F	
	31. Repression
16. T	
	32. Reaction formation
17. F	
18. T	33. Projective identification

34. Psychosexual

35. Oral

36. Anal expulsive

37. Phallic

38. Asceticism, Intellectualization

CHAPTER FIVE

1. T

2. F (Eight stages)

3. T

4. F (12 biological needs; 27 psychological needs)

5. F (Achievement)

6. T

7. F (They are <u>negatively</u> related)

8. T

9. F (Sullivan)

10. T (Westen)

11. T

12. T

13. T

14. T

15. F (Four distinct types: secure, avoidant, disorganized, ambivalent)

16. T

17. Individuation

18. Psychosocial

19. Press

20. Power

21. Competence

22. Security operations

23. Splitting

24. Patriarchal, matriarchal

25. Avoidant

1. F (Latent content)

2. T

3. T

4. T

5. T

6. F (Resistance is an integral aspect of treatment)

7. T

8. T

9. T

10. T

11. T

12. F (He wrote about only 12 cases)

13. F

14. Manifest content, latent content

15. Sexual intercourse

16. Projective

17. Catharsis

18. Counter-transference

19. Vaginal (He was wrong; clitoral orgasm characterizes sexually mature women)

CHAPTER SEVEN

1. T

2. F (Facets are <u>narrow</u> aspects of personality)

3. T

4. F (Additive)

5. T

6. T

7. T

8. F (Normally distributed)

9. T

10. T

11. Sanguine (hopeful), melancholic (sad), choleric (hot-tempered), phlegmatic (apathetic)

12. Facet

13. Convergent validity, discriminant validity

CHAPTER EIGHT

1.	F (Allport)	21. Lexical
2.	T	22. Central
3.	F (Cardinal)	23. L-data,
		Q-data,
4.	T	T-data
5.	F (Two types)	24. Correlation
		matrix
6.	F (Apparent in	
	school-age	25. Source
	children)	traits

1. F (Allport)
2. T
3. F (Cardinal)
4. T
5. F (Two types)
6. F (Apparent in school-age children)
7. T
8. F (Five steps)
9. T
10. F (Factor B)
11. F (P-E-N)
12. F (Jung)
13. T
14. F (Seven factors in Tellegen's model)
15. F (DSM)
16. F (Related to both)
17. T
18. F (Openness)
19. F (Least heritable)
20. T

21. Lexical
22. Central
23. L-data, Q-data, T-data
24. Correlation matrix
25. Source traits
26. Psychoticism Extraversion Neuroticism
27. Neuroticism Extraversion Openness Agreeableness Conscientiousness
28. DSM
29. Conscientiousness

CHAPTER NINE

1. F (Kretschmer)

2. F (Mesomorphs
   are
   muscular)

3. T

4. F (Synapse)

5. F

6. T

7. F

8. F (Only 1
   in 100)

9. F (Phenotypes)

10. T

11. F (0-1.00)

12. T

13. T

14. F (Less physical,
    just as verbal)

15. T

16. F (Inherited
    genotype;
    phenotype
    controlled by
    diet)

17. F (Father-absence
    affects both
    sexes; Eysenck
    believed it was
    heritable)

18. Ectomorph

19. Sympathetic
    parasympathetic

20. Synapes

21. Androgens
    estrogens

22. Assortative
    mating

23. 23

24. Concordance

25. Emotionality
    activity level
    sociability

CHAPTER TEN

1. F (Permitted; needs of state may "burden" right of privacy)

2. F (Five)

3. F (30)

4. T

5. F (2 million people took the MBTI in 1990)

6. T

7. T

8. T

9. T

10. F (Is effective in some cases)

11. F (May temporarily relieve depression)

12. T

13. T

14. T

15. T

16. T

17. F (Criticized by Block)

18. T

19. Myers-Briggs Type Indicator

20. GSR

21. Neuroleptics (Antipsychotics)

22. Endorphins

23. Cynical hostility

CHAPTER ELEVEN

1. F (Overt)

2. T

3. T

4. F (Radical behaviorism)

5. F (Pairing of CS and UCS; focus on antecedents)

6. T

7. T

8. F (highly controlled)

9. F (minimum of constructs)

10. F (Direct observation)

11. F (Behavior therapy)

12. F

13. F ("Homework" is common)

14. Radical behaviorism

15. Classical conditioning, operant conditioning, observational learning (or modeling)

16. Behavior therapy

1. F (By accident; banned introspection)

2. T

3. T (Spontaneous recovery)

4. F (Up to 1 hour if taste is associated with illness)

5. T

6. F (Opposite processes)

7. T

8. F (Operant)

9. F (Favored cumulative records to depict changes in response rate)

10. F (Negative reinforcement is _removing_ an aversive stimulus; positive reinforcement in _presenting_ a rewarding stimulus)

11. F (Three phases at minimum)

12. F (Fixed-interval)

13. T

14. T

15. F (discrimination)

16. F (Opposite is true)

17. Introspection

18. Generalization gradient

19. Nocebo

20. Drug-mimicking; drug-mirroring

21. Extinction

22. Single-subject reversal design

23. Prompting and shaping

24. Fixed-interval, fixed-ratio, variable-interval, variable-ratio

25. Matching theory (Herrnstein)

CHAPTER THIRTEEN

1. T
2. T
3. T
4. T
5. F
6. T
7. T
8. T (Dilution effect)
9. F
10. F (Authoritarian)
11. F (Financial, human, social)
12. F (In some cultures it means "up yours")
13. T
14. Miller and Dollard
15. Information value
16. Androgynous
17. Dilution effect
18. Acceptance-involvement; strictness-supervision
19. Financial, human, social
20. Emblems
21. Activity settings

CHAPTER FOURTEEN

1. F (Mowrer and Mowrer)

2. T

3. F

4. F

5. T

6. T

7. F

8. T

9. F (Mastery model)

10. F (Criticized for being atheoretical)

11. T

12. F

13. Nocturnal enuresis

14. Aversion therapy

15. Premack principle

16. Response cost

17. Skill deficits, fear

18. Affirming the consequent

19. Situational tests

CHAPTER FIFTEEN

1. T	13. Internal frame of refrence
2. T	14. Humanism
3. F (Represent-ational Strategy)	15. Festinger
4. F (Rogers, Maslow)	16. Here-and-now
5. T	17. Existential psychology
6. F (here-and-now)	18. Empathy
7. F (idiothetic)	
8. F (Rollo May)	
9. F (Empathy)	
10. F (Free will, self-determination)	
11. F	
12. T	

1. F

2. F (Most valuable when <u>unconditional</u>)

3. T

4. F (There are five, but the <u>highest</u> is self-actualization)

5. F (Deficit motivation)

6. T

7. T

8. T

9. T

10. F (Always dichotomous)

11. T

12. T

13. T

14. Actualizing tendency

15. Organismic valuing process

16. Conditional positive regard

17. Conditions of worth

18. actual self, ideal self

19. Actual self-concept; undesirable self-concept

20. Threat

21. Perceptual distortion; denial

22. Reintegration

23. Person-centered approach

24. Physiological; safety; belongingness and love; esteem, self-actualization

25. Esteem from others; self-esteem

26. Growth motivation

27. Peak experience

28. Flow

29. Constructive alternativism

30. Predictive efficiency

31. Individuality corollary

32. Anxiety

33. Guilt

1. T
2. T
3. T
4. F (Independent; one can be high and the other at or near zero)
5. F (Generalized)
6. F (They are positively correlated)
7. F (Become <u>less</u> internal; return to predivorce level over time)
8. F (Behaviorist)
9. F (The two can be very different)
10: F (High internals may over-estimate their self- control)
11. T
12. F (Situation-specific)
13. T
14. F (Other way around)
15. F (opposite is true)
16. T

17. T
18. T
19. F (never discussed by Rogers)
20. F (<u>Decreases</u> chances of successs)
21. F (A degree of self-delusion appears to be adaptive)
22. T
23. F (Five broad classes)
24. Specific and generalized
25. Behavior potential
26. Person variables
27. Outcome expectancies
28. Consistency paradox
29. Prototypes
30. Schematic; aschematic
31. Material; social; spiritual
32. Negative "spillover"
33. Self-enhancement
34. Mood-congruent bias
35. Equifinality

CHAPTER EIGHTEEN

1. T

2. T

3. F (Rep test)

4. T

5. F (I-E scale)

6. T

7. F (Empathic understanding)

8. T

9. F (Kelly)

10. T

11. F (Modeling is more effective)

12. F

13. T

14. F (D'Zurilla and Goldfried)

15. F

16. T

17. T

18. T.

19. T

20. Q-sort

21. Rep test

22. Person-centered

23. Fixed-role therapy

24. Behavioral avoidance test

25. Naloxone

26. D'Zurilla and Goldried

27. Caring-days technique

CHAPTER NINETEEN

1. T
2. F
3. F
4. T
5. F
6. F
7. F
8. F (idiothetic)
9. T
10. T
11. F

12. Operating
    process;
    monitoring
    process

13. Environmental;
    Representational

14. Idiothetic

MATCHING THEORISTS AND THEIR IDEAS
PART II --PSYCHOANALYTIC

1.	f	13.	p
2.	i	14.	o
3.	i	15.	l
4.	e	16.	p
5.	e	17.	h
6.	f	18.	k
7.	a	19.	d
8.	n	20.	b
9.	m	21.	c
10.	r	22.	f
11.	g	23.	f
12.	q	24.	o

MATCHING THEORISTS AND THEIR IDEAS
     PART III--DISPOSITIONAL

1. a   11. k

2. a   12. l

3. i   13. l

4. e   14. g

5. e   15. n

6. h   16. b

7. f˙   17. j

8. m   18. o

9. f   19. c

10. e   20. d

MATCHING THEORISTS AND THEIR IDEAS
     PART IV--ENVIRONMENTAL

1. h   6. d

2. g   7. a

3. f   8. b

4. c   9. e

5. g   10. i

MATCHING THEORISTS AND THEIR IDEAS
PART V--REPRESENTATIONAL

1.	d	10.	d
2.	h	11.	l
3.	k	12.	a
4.	j	13.	i
5.	g	14.	i
6.	g	15.	i
7.	g	16.	f
8.	b	17.	c
9.	d	18.	e

MATCHING ASSESSMENT PROCEDURES AND THEIR CREATORS/USERS

1.	f	5.	c
2.	e	6.	a
3.	h	7.	d
4.	b	8.	g